SURFBOARDS

Luke Egan

Billabong.

Quiksilver
QUIK SiLVES
Quiksilver
Quiksilver

Quik

QUIK.

quiksilver

RY CRAIKE
RY CRAIKE
RY CRAIKE
RY
RY CRAIKE

ry craike

RY CRAIKE

ry craike

QUIK.
SILVER

QUIK.

uksilver

QUIKS

Quiksilver

quiksilver.com

the Search

RIP CURL

This book and the associated film, Transmission, are the results of a lifelong dream. For the past 20 years I've been travelling the world surfing and having fun with my friends, but I've always thought of doing the ultimate surf trip - the best waves, the best boat, the best friends, the best boards, the best time.

One of the coolest things in life is having dreams. The one thing cooler than that is when your dreams come true, when you make that dream become reality.

The first dream for me to come true was when I became a professional surfer. The second realisation of a dream was to make a good living at being that professional surfer. After fulfilling those couple of dreams I had confidence that if you work hard enough dreams can become reality. The key to this is believing it can happen. If you get as addicted to this as much as I have it becomes a credo for life - dream your dreams, live your dreams.

That's why this trip came about. I was on a trip last year on the Pelagic, a boat built by two surf-mad guys from California, Muz and Griff. It is the first of its kind - a boat specifically designed and built to go surfing. There are a lot of great boats out there, but not many that from when the pencil first hit the drawing board the major priority was to accommodate surfers and to search for and ride perfect waves. It was also built in Australia so for me it already had a spirit that I really related to and I knew it was the boat for this trip.

We had the Pelagic for 26 days, long enough to get some good waves around Indonesia. It was a big project to organise, but things started to evolve well. Some people couldn't make it for what ever reasons - hey, I tell you what, it's hard to get 18 of the top surfers in the world to sort out their itineraries so they can work around families, sponsorship commitments etc and go surfing in Indo with their mates for a couple of weeks - but this trip was one of my life's great experiences. Travelling with close friends who share the same interests and same desires - to surf perfect uncrowded waves, work on your boards with no distractions and just have some good quality time with the ocean.

I wanted to document the whole thing through a movie and a book. I didn't want it to be a documentary of my life, I just wanted to convey the joy of surfing great waves with great friends. Simple.

This book is something that I wanted to do for so long, something which is pure surfing and that's why I approached Reggae about Surfing World publishing the book. Most other surfing mags these days seem to get caught up in the commercial, competitive side of surfing. It's all about how much money someone is making, writers or people in the industry having a go at each other, who and what is cool, who's not or someone's opinion on who is the best surfer in the world.

Don't get me wrong I have been a part of all that, but I just wanted a change. It's almost taking a step backwards so I could go forward and really enjoy the reasons I became a surfer: to go surfing with my friends in a dream situation with everything being in the right place for all the right reasons.

It was an honour to have Jon Frank in charge of the still photographs. To me he is a purist photographer, his imagination is expressed in his photos and he makes his shots almost speak to you. When Ted Grambeau wanted to come on the second half of the trip it only enhanced what we wanted to achieve.

For the above reasons we decided that there would be no text with this book, other than this foreword, so Jon and Ted's photos could tell the story. Let the pictures from these great photographers take you on the journey and enjoy this book for all the reasons you started your love affair with surfing.

Go surfing. Surfing is a constant journey, looking for perfect waves. It seems to me the more perfect the waves you ride, the longer the journey gets. - **LUKE EGAN**

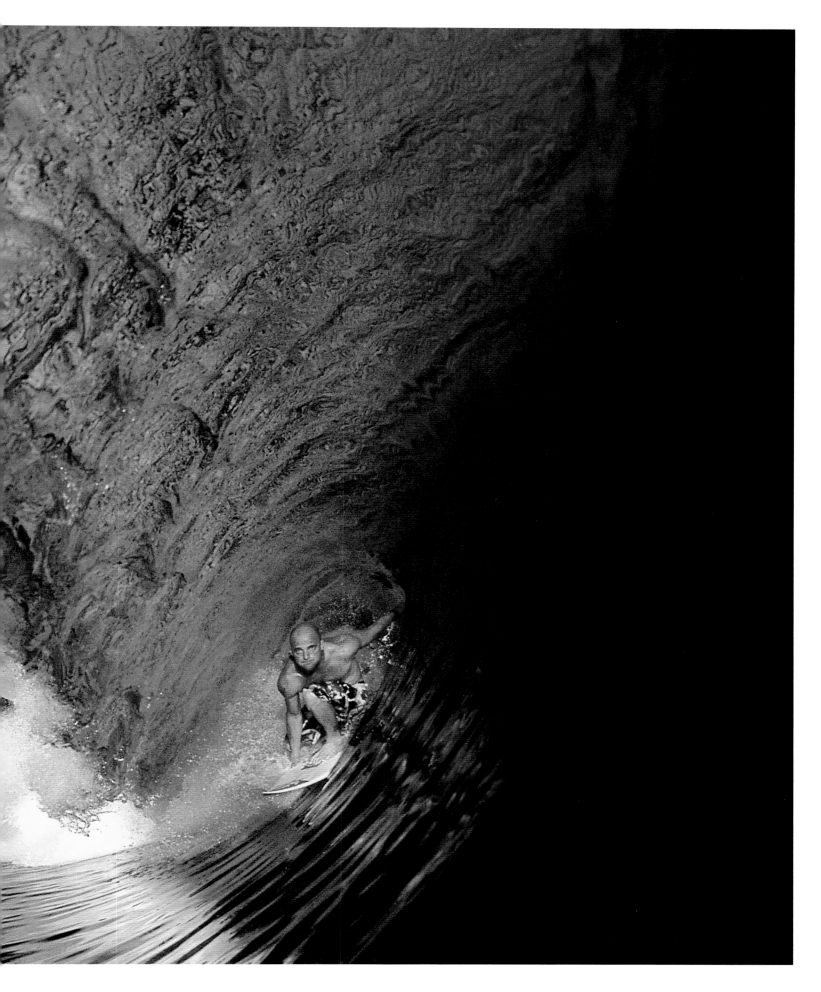

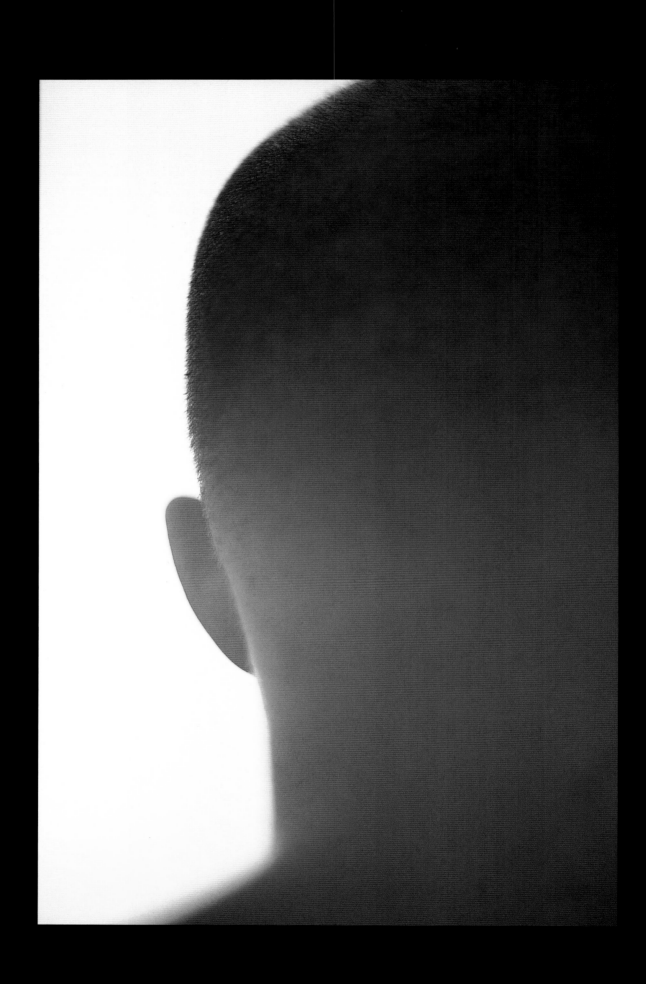

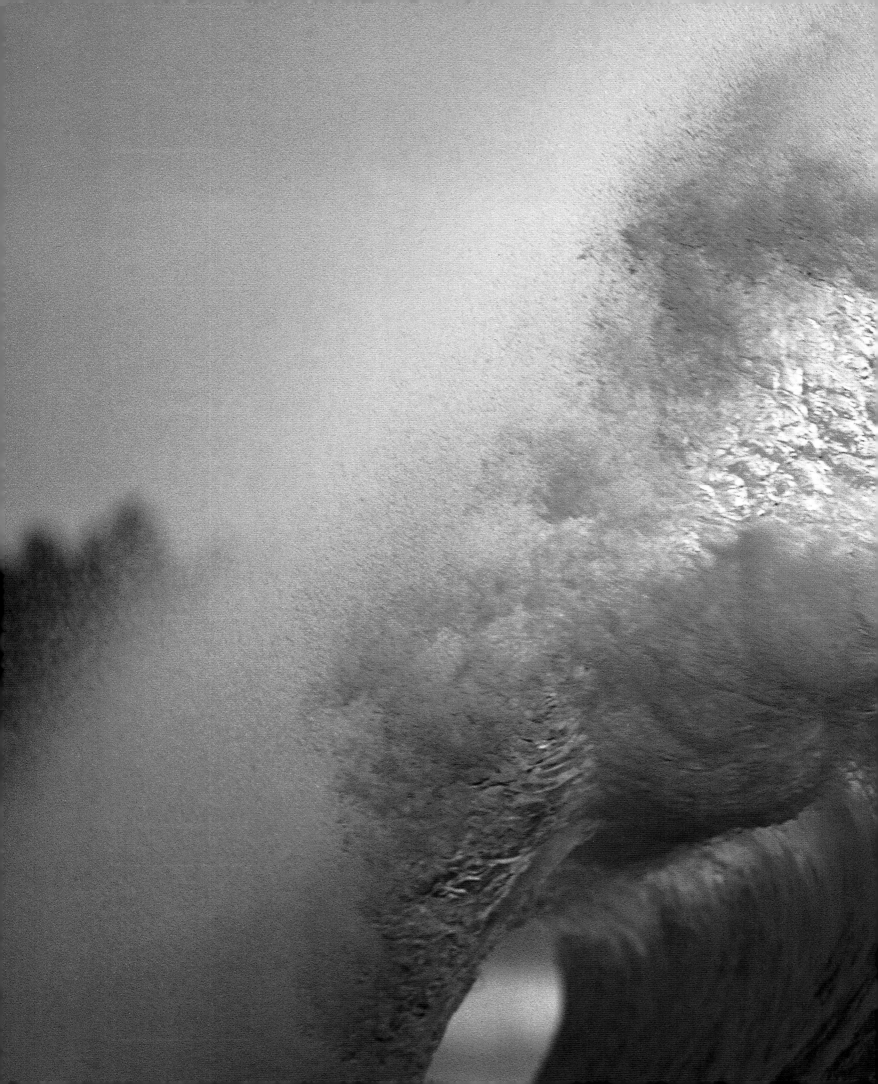

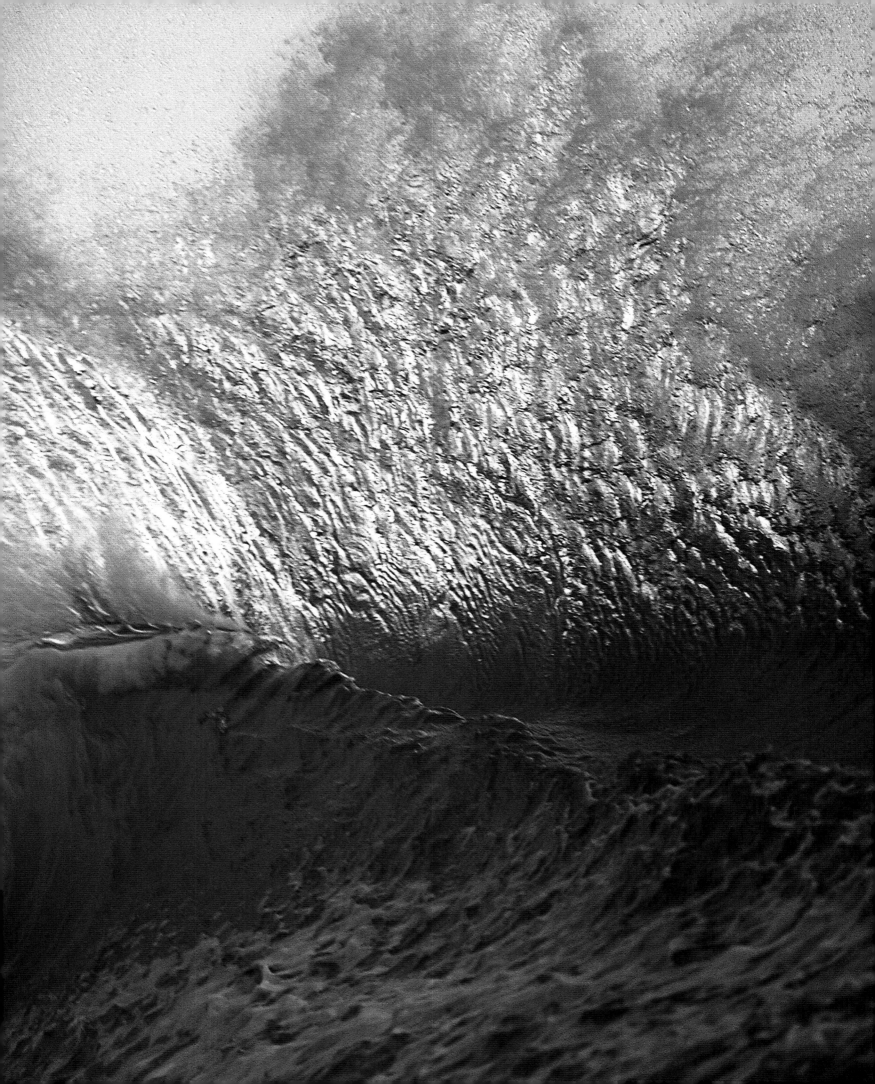

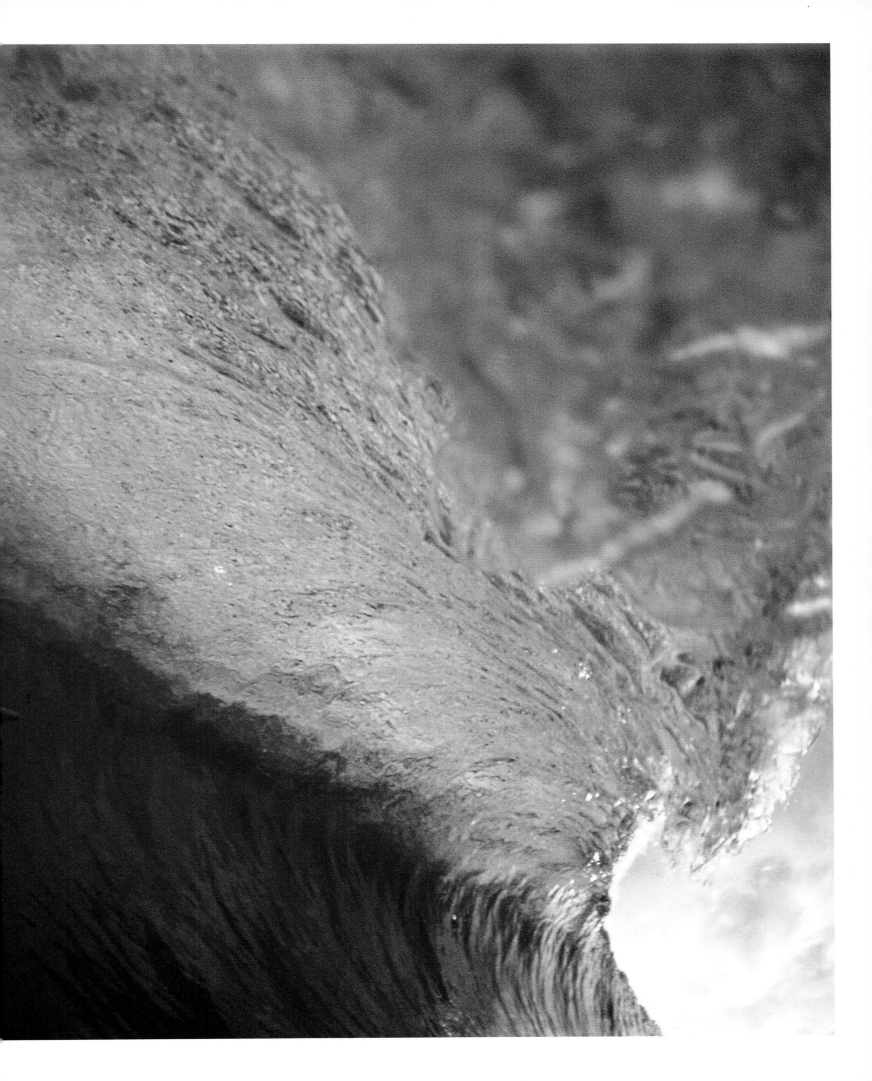

CREDITS

+ CONCEPT Luke Egan + EDITOR Reggae Elliss//reggaee@bigpond.com + ART DIRECTOR Mat Graham//gforcemessiah@bigpond.com
+ PHOTOGRAPHERS Jon Frank // Ted Grambeau + PHOTO EDITORS Jon Frank // Reggae Elliss // Mat Graham
+ ADVERTISING Doug Lees//dmlees@optusnet.com.au Ph: 0405 100044

+ Published by Breaker Publications Pty Limited, ACN 080 629 518, PO Box 747, Manly, NSW 2095.
Phone: (02)94009596. Transmission is Printed by Penfold Buscombe. Scanning by Nuscan. Distributed by Gordon and Gotch.

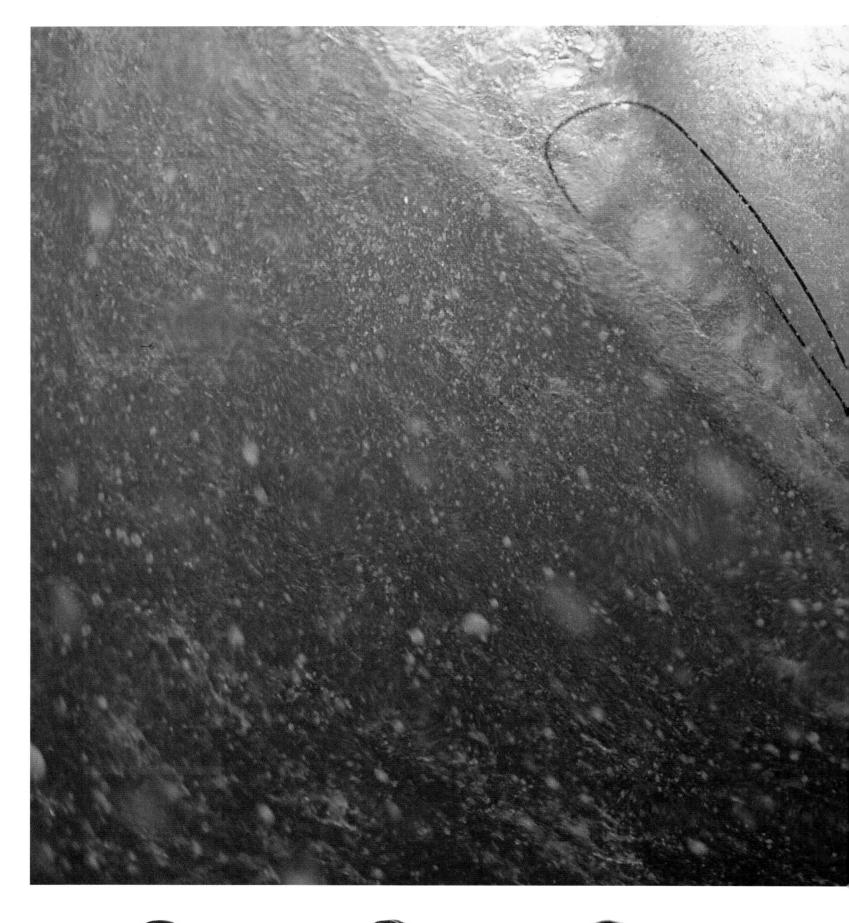

VEGA BLACK

VEGA COFFEE

VEGA KHAKI

LUKE EGAN

PHOTOS:AKILA AIPA_LUKE EGAN_JODY PERRY